STREET GLORY
THE UNTOLD STORY

STREET GLORY
THE UNTOLD STORY

AARON WELCH

MISSION POSSIBLE PRESS

Creating Legacies through Absolute Good Works

The Mission is Possible.

Sharing love and wisdom for the young and "the young at heart," expanding minds, restoring kindness through good thoughts, feelings, and attitudes is our intent. May you thrive and be good in all you are and all you do...

Be Cause U.R. Absolute Good!

Street Glory, The Untold Story © 2019 by Aaron Lamont Welch

No part of this book may be reproduced in any written, electronic, recording, or photocopying form without written permission of the publisher. The exception would be in the case of brief quotations embodied in critical articles or reviews and pages where permission is specifically granted by the publisher.

Although every precaution has been taken to verify the accuracy of the information contained herein, the author and publisher assume no responsibility for any errors or omissions. No liability is assumed for damages that may result from the use of information contained within.

Scripture taken from the Holy Bible, English Standard Version. ESV® Text Edition: 2016. Copyright © 2001 by Crossway Bibles, a publishing ministry of Good News Publishers. Used by permission. All rights reserved worldwide.

Books may be purchased in quantity by contacting the publisher directly:

Mission Possible Press, A division of Absolute Good,

PO Box 8039 St. Louis, MO 63156

or by calling 240.644.2500

MissionPossiblePress.com

ISBN: 978-0-9996766-6-0

First Edition   Printed in the United States

Dedication

This book is dedicated to my beautiful dear, praying grandmother, Ms. Beatrice Welch, who is 94 years old; to my lovely mother, the late Ms. Odessa Welch, who always made a way for her children; and to my brother, the late Michael Welch, Sr., who did his best being the man of the house when we were younger.

Acknowledgements

I would like to thank my daughters for being the joy in my life and for showing me how to be a stand-up father.

Thanks to my brothers and sisters for being my encouragement in life.

Thanks to Team No Lackin' for believing in our dreams.

Thanks to Ms. Jo Lena Johnson for being my writing coach, a good friend and for inspiring me to tell my story.

Contents

Growing Up 1
The Hustle 5
Boo, the Ladies Man 10
Treachery 18
The Break In 23
Warning Signs 29
Ambushed 34
Game Changing 38
Being a Husband 46
Big A and Lil' A 51
Hardworking Momma 61
Love and Loss 67
Becoming Homeless 71
Epilogue 82
Discussion 86
Fatherhood 87
Being Married 90
God's Grace 92
About the Author 96

"When you're making money, you feel like you can do whatever..."

Growing Up

"Dad, mom and a house full of kids, at first, that is."

Both of my parents were born in the South. Marianna, Arkansas is where my dad, Aaron, was born in 1938. I believe he moved to St. Louis for work, eventually landing at General Motors (GM), staying until he retired. My mother, Odessa, was born in Greenwood, Mississippi in 1940. My grandfather found better employment in Missouri so he moved his wife and their 12 children to St. Louis, where they planted roots and started their own families.

My oldest sister was born in 1961, when my mom was about 21 years old. I was born in 1969, the fifth of seven children born to my mother. Back in the early 70s when we were growing up, we lived on the North Side of St. Louis, in the Walnut Park area in a two-family flat, with both of my parents. At that time, it was a nice neighborhood, mixed with whites and Blacks. Our mom was a mother figure to all the neighborhood kids, taking them in when they needed it and disciplining them like they were her own. If you got out of line, she would spank you with a switch. To this day, when I see some of my childhood friends, they tell me how much they appreciated and respected her for guiding them down a better path.

On Our Own

When I was about six or seven, my dad and mom split up so we moved to the West Side, into Savoy Court, an apartment complex close to Delmar and Union in St. Louis City. That was about the time I lost contact with my dad. Our mother was a hardworking, lovable woman who began working two jobs to provide for us. Her primary job was at a rehabilitation center in Bellefontaine, Missouri, a suburb in St. Louis' North County. She dispensed medicine to mentally ill patients for over 30 years until she retired. Her "second jobs" rotated but were all in the nursing field.

After my oldest sister (Niecy) left home, that's when Lynn, the second oldest, became a second mother to the rest of us. My mother was an excellent cook who knew how to prepare meals out of whatever she had. When Lynn was in charge my sister cooked, made sure our school work was done and made sure we were properly bathed. This went on until she met and married her husband, a good man who I'm proud to call brother-in-law.

We grew up attending LoveJoy Missionary Baptist Church. As the months and years went by, my older brother, Michael, found Christ and became the man of the house, as he was next in line. He took responsibility for things and made sure we did our chores. He also took time to teach us, his three younger brothers, what manhood was about, at an early age. He walked us and our sister, Renee to school and picked us up, because we were too young to go back and forth on our own. Around that time, we all got more involved in church and even joined the choir, which I actually enjoyed. That was a good time in our lives. When Michael moved out, I quit singing in the church choir, as I didn't want to be perceived as soft.

> *"Each time a family member left, it affected us and took us in a new direction. I often wonder what life would have been like if my parents had not split up."*

The Hustle

"With my older brother, Michael out of the house, I became the next 'man of the house' though I was only a young teenager."

My interests started changing and I saw plenty of things on-screen and in the streets I liked and wanted. Two of my favorite movies were *Super Fly* and *The Mack* because I was impressed with the hustling skills, the cars, the women and that lifestyle. Those movies were "classics" by that time, the mid 80s, but the impression they made was unforgettable. I was also a big fan of the TV show, *Miami Vice* where almost every episode was drug-related. Though the main characters of the show were cops, I loved their style. I also loved the idea of making quick, fast money. I was getting deeply involved in the street life, becoming a street guy/hustler. Money, popularity, fame, big houses, cars, jewelry, women and power were enticing. The thought of being in control of a dynasty like Al Pacino's character in *Scarface* hooked me.

High School

When I was a freshman attending Sumner High School, I wore Stacy Adams shoes, Leading Men plaid slacks with the matching leather jacket and carried a brief case that matched my shoes. I had a long Jheri Curl and I was fly. There was a beautiful young lady who happened to be a junior. She liked me and wasn't afraid to show it, especially when she stopped by my locker to run her fingers through my hair. I liked the attention but nothing happened between me and the young lady because I was expelled after an upperclassman who liked her got jealous and started a fight with me that I finished. Between my fist and the combination lock that was in it, it was lights out for him and being put out for me. Less than a week after school started, I was gone.

I started attending Riverview Gardens Senior High, as I was sent "out to the County" to live with my aunt and cousins to keep me out of trouble. That helped a little bit but not a lot, because I was making my money on the weekends back on the West Side on the Hodiamont Tracks and in the Cabanne Courts projects. I met a guy named Red who became my first friend and introduced me to others. After school I would hang out in Castle Point, Moline Acres and Hathaway Manor – all little neighborhoods in the school district. Being a new kid at school, I was pretty much quiet, but I was still fly. I kept my business to myself and nobody there knew what I did to dress so well.

I started taking boxing lessons at the Wohl Center, a historic place where Black kids have found safety and shelter for many years. Boxing helped me to focus and took a few hours a week out of my hustle game – but it also developed my punching skills which would come in handy during the many street fights me and my boys would get involved in.

The times and styles were changing. As soon as I turned 16 I got my driver's license and my brother, Michael gave me his wine-colored '76 Buick Regal with a tan top and white walls. I had a booming system with 6x9 speakers and a cassette player with a one-touch ejection button installed. Being mobile made it easier for me to run my budding enterprise.

I had to get the Billy Jean and Thriller jackets to emulate the Michael Jackson looks. Being a trendsetter, I got rid of the Curl and I got my hair cut into a box with a long tail. That's what people were doing in California and when I saw it on Ozone, a character in the movie *Breakin'*, I knew I had to do it too. The County had some good shopping including Northland Shopping Center and I was a frequent spender at Jeans West in River Roads Mall where I bought the hippest, most stylish clothes...

I became a good Break Dancer, known for my pop lockin' skills. On those days I wore Parachute pants, the fat laced Adidas shell-toed shoes and Adidas jogging suits with fat gold chains and Kangol caps like LL Cool J, following the East Coast looks and trends. Argyle sweaters, paisley print shirts, heavily starched Levi's Jeans and penny loafers with quarters was what I wore on my preppy days.

> *"Being quiet about my personal life gave me a chance to stack my money, to provide and to look good while doing it. I was hooked on the hustle."*

Boo, the Ladies Man

"By sixteen I was mannish, charming the PYTs."

Screwing

I was hanging in the hood and noticed this young lady named Cindy. A PYT (pretty young thing), she was a year older than me, had a cute little body and a long ponytail with real pretty hair, which she got from her mother, who was Indian (Native American). She kept staring at me and then asked a couple of guys, who were mutual friends, who I was. Once I found out she was interested I smoothly made my approach. I gave her that killer conversation and we started "talkin." Having long conversations on the phone, knowing we had to be at school the next day was what we did during the week. We started seeing each other regularly on the weekends. We went from hugs to a peck on the cheek, a kiss on the lips, to holding each other and the next thing we knew, we were in the sheets. I was anxious to get it, to be one of the first guys in the neighborhood to get such a cute girl with that "Coke bottle shape." I was mannish and didn't even consider the consequences of getting her knocked up/pregnant.

I was scared the day she told me she missed her cycle. I was sixteen. I asked her what she wanted to do. Being the type of guy I was, I wasn't even going to consider abortion because I wanted to be there for my seed, something I produced in this world. Naturally she was scared and nervous too, but never considered not keeping the baby. Knowing our child was coming, but still being a street guy, I continued being secretive and also protective of her and her identity. I didn't want anyone to know who the mother of my child was, for their own good. Back then, when this went down, I was providing. I had the money and the means to take care of my growing family, and that it was. We had another daughter and then I had a third daughter. Right around that time I met Brenda.

Brenda

I was driving my army green 1993 Bronco with low profile rims when I met Brenda on the bus stop on Russell, on the South Side. I saw her standing there, immediately made a U-turn, got out and asked her if she was cold. She said yes, we exchanged numbers and I offered to take her home. She let me take her. I called her that same night and we talked on the phone. I asked her would she want to go out. We went to the show that Friday night and things went from there. As we continued dating, feelings started getting stronger between us. She was the first woman I fell in love with. During that time I was still living the street life. She was loyal to me and I could trust her to hold my money. After we started being intimate, she was the one woman who I couldn't get pregnant. I loved her and wanted a baby with her. She wasn't on birth control, but she never got pregnant. We continued seeing each other for about three years. I remember going to the nightclub called, "The Garage," where I ended up meeting Shonda, and that's how me and Brenda broke up.

Shonda

Shonda remembered me from our childhood, but I didn't remember her. As we started talking, we learned we stayed in the same hood but on the opposite ends of the street. We started seeing each other. I was quiet about that. One night Shonda came over to one of the sets (streets) I was on and Brenda was there. Shonda got out of the car. Brenda was looking like, "Who is this B?" and Shonda was looking like, "Who are you?" Shonda asked Brenda who she was and Brenda replied, "I'm his woman." It was ugly. They exchanged words then a couple of punches were thrown before I could get in between them. Once they were separated, they both asked who I was going to be with. I chose

Shonda because I hadn't slept with her yet. Brenda got in the car with her friends and drove off. It hurt for me to see Brenda leave, but I made my choice. Though I was in love with Brenda, I chose Shonda that night. It was dumb of me to let someone who had my back go all for the thrill of having new sex. It took a week or so and Shonda and I did it. It was good but wasn't worth me losing Brenda for a piece of tail.

I called myself letting things die down before I called Brenda a few weeks later. I apologized and told her that I really loved her and was sorry for hurting her. But it was a little too late because she had already gotten with someone else. I got a call that Brenda was on Vandeventer and Kennerly with another guy, I lost it. I raced over to where they were and confronted her, "Who is this n*gga?" I could see she was scared. She knew my history and background. She was quiet. I then exchanged words with the dude. He got in my face. We tussled, threw some punches and he ended up cracking the windshield of his Cadillac with the force of his body, of which I provided the momentum. It was another dumb move, but I was in love and angry. That night, Brenda chose. She left with him. What goes around comes around. It's funny. I considered myself such a ladies' man. But when the tables were turned, I couldn't deal seeing the person I was loving in the arms of another man.

Surrounded by Females

I'm not bragging on this, I'm just being honest… I was living the life and women came with the territory. I had three daughters by the time I was 19 years old, and was taking care of their needs, and their mother's needs as well.

Fatherhood, even at that early age changed me. It turned me into a man, or what I thought being a man was about, because I grew up without a father in my life and I was determined to always be present for my own children. Being a dad who was responsible meant that I played with them, took pictures with them, took them shopping, played in the park, took them to carnivals and was always present at birthdays and special occasions. I was making time for them in my entrepreneurial schedule. But my business was growing, I wasn't trying to miss out on money either. I was putting in the time in my business and I was putting in the time as a ladies' man – it all came with the territory. This meant I was getting more involved with other women. It worked out pretty well because as long as they were getting what they needed, they didn't complain. They were young too, so what they "needed" at that time was money, keeping their hairstyles up to date, jewelry, Aigner riding boots with matching belts, plaid pants and those ruffle shirts. They all had the Queen Latifah/Monie Love looks with Nefertiti on their herringbone necklaces when they weren't wearing their add-a-bead chains and dolphin earrings.

The song "As We Lay" by Shirley Murdock was the song back then. I remember being on the telephone and one of my girls played that song to me. It was cute, talking about getting together over the phone. It didn't take long before we ended up doing it. Sleeping around back then wasn't cool but it was acceptable, given the times and our ages. We didn't even talk about if they were on the pill or not. And I was acting in the heat of the moment, feeling so good, I didn't take the precautions necessary to prevent pregnancy. We had sex education in school. I knew about chlamydia and gonorrhea. We didn't worry about the diseases and things like we have to today. I had a lot of choices with the ladies but many of them I was just "cool with." And there were certain ones I wanted to be intimate with. I was charming to the ladies and they were getting what they wanted and I was getting what I wanted. It all worked out, in the sense that I have five beautiful daughters. I love them, I'm proud of them, and I have always been in their lives.

> *"As I matured, and after I got married, I stopped being a ladies' man. I'm proud of that, but it took a while to get there."*

Treachery

"My heart died and I was lost. I was confused in this world, but you couldn't tell me that."

Although the street life seemed glamorous, especially when bringing in more money in a week than most people made in a year, the cost was high. The movie *Colors* came out in 1988, just as I was graduating high school. We saw the LA street gangs and how they were doing things. That exposure influenced us all around the country and St. Louis was no exception. Around 1990 products were changing, becoming more addictive and more potent. The game was changing too, becoming more violent and heavy. People were becoming more ruthless and bold, listening to certain Gangsta rap artists and thinking they could pull off what they were hearing made our streets deadly.

Carnage

When I was in my early 20s, I had a couple of my darkest days. With our pagers on our hips, we used pay phones when we needed to make a call or get a message, just as they did in *New Jack City*. I will never forget the day of my 20th birthday. I was on the set off Cote Brilliante and got a *911* page. When I returned the page/made the call I found out my friend had been killed. I sped off in my blue Caprice Classic and I arrived on the scene, but his body had already been removed. I felt the pain of losing someone who was like family. It was surreal, hurtful until I saw him in the casket at his funeral. As I walked toward his body, seeing him lay there, a pain shot through me. I thought about the good times we had, running up and down Halls Ferry Road, rapping to "*La Di Da Di*" mimicking Doug E. Fresh and Slick Rick during our younger days. I questioned if living the street life was worth it but I had too many mouths to feed to let it go. I shed some tears and I paid my respects as I said goodbye. I still think of him every year on my birthday.

One afternoon me and a few of the guys in my crew were standing on the street chatting it up. We noticed a car starting to slow down as it approached my boy Mickey. As they did the drive-by, they shot him in his head as he was standing outside his car about 100 feet away from me. As soon as the shots were fired, I ran to him. Much like the scene in *Boyz in the Hood*, I held him as he died in my arms.

The ambulance came on the scene, along with the police, asking questions. We didn't give them answers, period. I was devastated, angry and I wanted revenge. Everyone was angry and confused, wanting to know what happened. I was in shock. It was horrifying. Nobody was expecting anything like that to happen. It was the first time we witnessed a friend being murdered.

The day Mickey's blood seeped through my clothes changed me completely. To see someone get shot before my eyes. It made me more cautious and more aware of my surroundings. It also made me look at things totally different, more serious in my observations of people. I was scared, hurt and became hardened all in the same moment. I made sure not to let strangers get too close to me after that yet, seeing Mickey like that didn't stop me from hustling.

We never found out who the guy was who pulled the trigger that day, in broad daylight, for all of us to witness. We know it wasn't enterprise related because if it had been, the truth would have come out eventually. To this day we don't know if it was jealousy, as we were all driving rag top Cadillacs on 30s and Vogue tires, with kits on the back at the time, or if it was over a female. We will never know. Back then every hood had their G (Loyalty) code they lived by, "If one falls, we all fall together." Today, no one is living by that or any code, really; if one falls, he's snitching on the other man. The game was meant to be told not sold, nowadays everybody's sellin' and tellin.'

"Street Glory... It's all sad really. So many young lives were lost and so many babies became orphans before their fathers really became men."

The Break In

"In 1996 the song 'Captain Save a Hoe' by E-40 was out and I was out there saving some of everybody."

I rented a house on Kensington, on the West Side. I had been living there and operating my business for about two years with no problem. It was a quiet life with my girl, Candace, who I loved.

The day they broke into the house, it was about 3 or 4 in the morning. Candace and I were asleep when I heard something rattling at the door. I wasn't sure what it was and kind of laid there listening. When I heard something pop, it was too late, two guys were already in the house with guns pointed to our heads. One scared Candace badly as he was yelling at her, "Where's the money?" Petrified, she cried and told him she didn't know. She didn't. I hadn't told her.

As the other guy began ransacking the room, they dared me to move, knowing I wouldn't, with her life in jeopardy, one bullet to the head between life and death. As he was yelling, Candace was shaking so badly, I was ready for him to kill me, just to make sure he didn't kill her. At first I wouldn't tell him anything but when I saw he was desperate enough to kill her, I told him to open the dresser, which had two hidden doors. They got most of the jewelry I had just had made and many other items with a high-street value. That night they took me for more than $20k, which included $7,000 worth of jewelry and $3,500 in cash. There was more in the house but they were satisfied with their take and ran out of the front door. They thought they had gotten off, scot-free. They didn't. As one of the guys was demanding money, I immediately recognized his voice. He was someone who I was helping to get established and get on his own two feet. I guess what I was doing for him was not enough, since he and his boy broke into my house and held us at gunpoint. But that's what comes with the territory when you are living that street life.

Once they left I grabbed my weapon and then I grabbed Candace to try and calm her down. That didn't really help. She was too shaken and frightened. I had put her life in jeopardy. She had wanted the life but wasn't prepared for the consequences of the life. She called her friend and told her she was coming to her house. She continued to cry as she stormed out, with her children in tow. Grateful that the kids were not discovered and slept through the whole ordeal, I understood what she did and why. I didn't try to stop her from leaving, I just wanted them safe at that point.

Empty House

I was a laid back guy who kept a low profile until I started dealing with the wrong people. After that strong-arm robbery, I was ready for war. I immediately got on the phone and told my people what happened. They arrived, 10 cars deep and with people riding in the back of the U-Haul, ready for battle. When they arrived, you would have thought they were Mexican bandits (no offense to my brown brothers). As I was waiting for them I had secured all my remaining valuables. We packed up all of the furniture except my bed and a few of my clothes. In a couple of hours everything was tucked away in storage. When we finished at the storage place, we came back and cleared the street. We had to get answers and we got the answers. People started pointing and talking. Some who had heard what was going on confirmed that who I thought it was, was correct. We didn't find out who his partner was, but I was ready for him.

I stayed at the house, on guard with a box spring and mattress, protecting what was mine. Candace, still extremely shaken, had been sleeping at her mother's house. Three days later is when she left me – officially, and for good. The day after I lost my woman, I was driving down Clarendon and saw the thief walking along the Hodiamont Tracks. I immediately jumped out of my car and used my boxing skills, along with my slugger. Let's just say, he never had to worry about where he would take a dump again, it was always with him. I felt like I got justice.

I was missing Candace and the kids. I was alone in an empty house and I didn't like the feeling. I called her to see how she was doing. She talked but said she would never come back to me because she realized how dangerous the street life really was. I was hurt because the person I was loving I wasn't going to get back. I missed her, I can't act like I didn't. But I've always bounced back quickly. Though my feelings for Candace were stronger than I had felt for anyone else, as time proceeded, I started getting involved with other women. I liked women, they liked me and they weren't afraid of the lifestyle I was living. Some were attracted to the danger, some to the money and others to the fame of being a hustler's woman. They would be quick to brag, "I got me a baller, girl." That's what they would say, as I bought them all the Dooney & Burke and Coach purses they wanted. The life was attractive to them, and the power I had on the street was seductive. Yet, to this day, I feel like Candace was supposed to be my wife. It wasn't ever to be.

About two months later, I was still living the street life and I caught a case. I ended up on a four-year probation. I was fortunate that I only got probation because it could have been a 10-year sentence. One of the main reasons I believe I didn't get locked up was because I had always maintained a real job. Being a taxpayer actually helped.

> *"In 1996 my life flashed before my eyes and changed my whole world, but not my business endeavors."*

Warning Signs

"People and events were telling me to get out of the hustle. I heard them, but I wasn't listening."

Strangers

At the time, I drove a blue four-door Buick Century when someone ran into my car while parked on the street outside of my job at Lee's Chicken. It was totaled and I didn't have insurance on it. Nobody had it at that time, living that life. A man walked in and asked, "Did you call on someone?" I was off the clock and it took me a minute to respond. I said, "Yes, I called my brother-in-law to pick me up." Which was only true at that point because the accident had just happened. He asked me again, "Did you call on someone?"

By that time I realized he wasn't talking about a phone call. He then said, "Whatever you're going through, God is going to make sure you're okay." I had a strange feeling and knew what he was saying. It was confirmation from God because I had been saying to God that I would leave that lifestyle. Though, as I was riding the docket, going back and forth to court, I kept my job and I kept my business.

About a week later I saw him again. I happened to go to into the Aldi's at Page and Kingshighway. I had run in to get something and ended up in his line, not realizing who he was. He asked me the same question, "Did you call on someone?" And then he began telling me it was time to give my life back to Christ. When he said that I talked to him and said, "Thank you." As I shook his hand. I walked out and haven't seen him since.

About three weeks later, I was pumping gas at the Amoco station at Natural Bridge and Kingshighway when a lady came and put her hands on mine and said, "Whatever you are doing, stop what you are doing and give your attention to God." As she was walking away, it was as if she vanished in mid-air. When that happened I was in disbelief. And I knew that was another confirmation from God, telling me the same thing. I was raised in church. I knew what was right and wrong, even though I wasn't living like I should.

Undercover Brother

As I was leaving my house less than a month after the gas station appearance, a Black undercover agent said my name as I was getting into my car, "Aaron, get out the car."

My response was, "Who the f*ck are you?"

That's when he flashed his badge. He said, "Everybody who you think is your friend ain't your friend. I've been watching you for a while and from what I see, you're more of a family man. Take my advice and get out the game or you can get popped by someone else who won't give two flyin' f*ucks about you." When he said that, I looked at him then got in my car and drove off. Of course, that was another confirmation that my time in the game was up. I thought about it but wasn't ready to stop.

For a minute I played like I was out of the game but I wasn't. I just kept a lower profile, but I never forgot what he said about friends not being my friends. I was being more cautious and watched my surroundings. Me being as hard-headed as I am, I was still hustling and got jammed up again by some undercover agents. About four months later I was riding with Dee, one of my women. I was telling her which streets to take because she wanted to be seen since she had just gotten her new Suzuki Sidekick for which I had bought low-rider profile tires with a boomin' system. She took her route instead of the route I told her to take. When we got to the corner of Ashland and Fair, four undercover cars swarmed us. I was pissed. It was a serious situation which could have put me into prison. This is when I gave one of the greatest performances of my life. I never did drugs but I decided to act like I did so that they wouldn't arrest me and throw me in prison. I figured if I acted like I was strung out they would go light on me and seek help for me. I was sitting in the back of the police car and one of them asked me if I was okay. I told him I was and that I just needed something to get high with. I had studied many people who were on drugs and I just started mimicking their behavior. As they transported me downtown and told my probation officer what was going on (that I was addicted), he sent me to AA classes, that's what saved me from doing hard time.

> *"God said I'm not through with you yet. I knew those were my guardian angels."*

Ambushed

"I had a 1986 burgundy Grand Prix with a burgundy rag top on 30s and Vogue tires. It had 12-inch woofers, four 6x9 speakers on the back panel and four 4x9s on the doors with tweeters above the windshield. I was too busy making money to get my gas gauge fixed."

In 1997, I was living that nightmare all over again. When I was driving down Marcus and Lee with four pockets-full of money, I happened to run out of gas. I got on the pay phone as five guys came up to me with guns. One guy got $1,800 out of one pocket, another got $2,500 out of another pocket. As I was tussling with him at the payphone, my crew pulled up. Shots were fired. Everyone scattered, running in different directions. We never did catch the guys. My boys took me to get gas to fill up my car. Afterward, when I was back at the house in deep thought, I realized that I had angels protecting me, considering everything that had happened to me. There I was in that bare house alone, bruised and robbed of a lot but not all of my money, and I had another chance. But I didn't stop.

1998

After I got off papers, the game started changing. I was always the type that knew how to generate money in different ways. I kept a job, I paid my taxes, and I took care of my children. My life started changing. I found out the people I thought were my friends weren't my friends. You know, when you got it you got it. When the money is gone, they are gone. After six months, somehow, some way, I managed to gain back my fame. During that time I had a tougher organization. I had women working for me.

On Marcus and Martin Luther King, Nadine was my number one go-to girl. She was so smooth. No one ever knew she was living that life as well.

I had another house set up around the corner on Evans, and one further up on Cote Brilliante. I was living the lifestyle of a true hustler. I was running those three houses and everything was sewed up. During that time I had the money, the fame, the fortune and the ladies, four of them, to be exact. I was providing for them, giving them everything they needed and wanted. The only thing they wanted from me that I couldn't give them was my heart. Candace still had it but she didn't want it. Looking back on it, I hate I brought them all into that life.

As I was running the three houses that's when it hit me that the life wasn't for me anymore. I couldn't sleep, I had to look over my shoulders and I had to worry about who was going to try and hurt me next. When I saw my own family members become hooked, that's when I realized how I was destroying other family's lives. I didn't want that for my life. It was a game changer when it got too close to me. The life of a hustler. It took me a while but I was slowly getting out of that lifestyle. After getting so many confirmations from other people telling me to rededicate my life back to Christ, I knew it was just a matter of time before I would be taken out if I didn't give up what I had come to love, though I didn't trust it, the game, that is.

I started telling Nadine that I was ready to make a change and get out of the game. She said she didn't want to do it anymore either. For a minute I kind of slept on the products. And then started to clear out my inventory, selling it for less than the value. Nadine got out with me and we stayed together off and on for a few months but she wanted to go back to school and become a school teacher and felt it best to separate from me. Two of the others continued doing their thing and we lost touch. The fourth I didn't know well, it was just more of a sex thing. I heard later that she got caught up, using.

> *"By getting out of the game I felt relieved, like I could be free and could go places without having to look over my shoulders or worry about people hurting me or my family."*

Game Changing

"I got out, but it didn't last."

I continued working my tax payer jobs, but things weren't going as well as I hoped because though I had saved a little money from my enterprise, I was used to having a lot more. I had built up an extensive network of white clientele who trusted me and my product. They would get packages of 100, 500, or even 1000 capsules of *boy* at a time. When I had to rely on those small checks from my restaurant and retail jobs, I struggled. In my head I kept thinking, ***get back into it***. I was out of it for nearly six months. I wanted the material things the lifestyle brought and I couldn't resist getting back in. I did so but during that time the game had really changed. When I went back, my product wasn't the same, it was *girl* and my ultimate consumer was Black.

My business was about weight, I was a supplier, which meant I didn't interact with individuals too much. The middle man got what he needed from me, cut it, shared it, and then someone along the way provided it to the end user. That was a layer of insulation which kept me less affected by what my enterprise was doing to the overall neighborhoods. The only time I really interacted with individuals was when I needed the car washed, the house cleaned or a snack from High Rollers Mini Mart, the neighborhood store. I would pay them cash money or hook them up with a small amount of product. However, I didn't sell to them. That wasn't my business model. That was a good thing because I didn't have individuals coming around trying to buy, I had good relationships with many of them. If five-o came on the block, they would tell me and I would go into their houses, sit in the kitchen and wait for things to die down before going back out and continuing business.

We'd have dice games on the set, winning money and having fun times while others were doing any and everything to get the next fix.

Those on my level and didn't have much to worry about, it was good wholesome times in the neighborhood. I would buy bomb pops for all the kids in the neighborhood whenever they came around. I sometimes paid electric bills for families so their kids had a decent place to live, all while someone in their house was hooked and couldn't work to pay for it themselves. Fun times of course, included women. During that time when the money was good, we went down to the Freaknik every year, just to be part of that super-wild time. Seeing the women wilding, being nude in the streets and fun times. Everybody was at Freaknik.

I Snapped

One day I saw someone very close to me go into a neighbor's house. I knew what type of life he was living and that he was also a street guy. An older man, he would lure women in and have his way. Something snapped in me when I thought about what she was likely going to do for a $15 or $20 fix. Seeing that was about to tear my soul apart and I wasn't having it. I went to his door and confronted him. He was a little disturbed that I was interrupting his day-time adult plans but I didn't care. I grabbed him, dragged him off his porch and commenced to using my boxing skills. It was so bad that he moved out of the neighborhood. I was so incensed that my rage turned to numbness. It's almost like the years of living that lifestyle came down to those bloody moments. Thinking about it makes me upset because he did that to so many women in the neighborhood. I was seconds from blowing him away. My mother saw me almost take a man's life. She stepped in and said, "This is wrong. Don't do it. You will spend the rest of your life in jail if you do it."

I thought about it and said, "You're right mom."

My mother saved his life that day.

Out of Control

Afterward, I thought about what I had done to him and also what I had been doing to so many others. I never got sex in exchange for product – that wasn't my business. However, contributing to the habits of those who were addicted was a terrible thing and I guess I really didn't see it or care enough until it directly affected someone I cared about. I know I was being a hypocrite but I'm just grateful for maturity, age and knowing I had a responsibility to my children. I had to stop. I had been in business for so long and it was a difficult transition but it's like I lost all taste and tolerance for the game in that man's yard that day, after he was beat down.

Things were getting hot. I was controlling one area of Natural Bridge and a friend was controlling the other side. We had been doing big numbers for about two years, but things were getting too hot for us to continue and my heart wasn't in it. We came to an agreement to end our business ventures and parted ways to cover ourselves and each other.

That time, I got out of the game completely. I wanted a better life for me and to be able to look over my shoulder and not feel like I was in danger. To see how women were selling their bodies for a $15 or $20 piece of stone, kids with birth defects, speech impediments, addictions, and people overdosing, it was hurtful and painful for me to see and witness that. It changed me because I saw how I was destroying the lives of people's family members. Deep down inside I didn't have the desire or drive to live like that anymore. Even though I knew I was doing wrong, over the years it was hurting me to see how people were dressed in the same clothes without bathing, how their looks were fading because of addiction and seeing the things they were doing just to get a fix. It was hurting me in my soul to see how I was contributing to that with deadly products. As long as I was still doing it, I was damaging people's family's and this goes back to when the undercover brother said I could continue and get popped by someone who didn't care about me – I was changing for the better. I didn't want that life anymore.

Doing tricks for rocks, asking for favors. Starting to see how women wanted to lay with certain guys and how they wanted to have oral sex for a 20 dollar bill. I just wanted peace of mind and to have control of myself. Even though it was hard, I maintained by having two jobs. No one ever knew that I was working because of the image I kept up so well but I had to take care of my daughters.

I kept my daughters away from each other because of the way I was dealing with their mothers, until they were older. I wasn't in a relationship with them but I always provided for the girls and made sure their mom's didn't want for the things they needed.

As time passed, I felt I no longer had a curse on me – *"Somebody's Watching Me"* by Rockwell – it was probably my conscious – I felt bad about ruining the lives of human beings. I wanted to get away and have a clean slate and get out of the game. I felt like it was safe to get the girls together, and not be in danger, based on what I did. I wanted to be able to walk out of my door and feel like I would be alright.

"Ultimately, if people know where the weight was coming from, they would have probably wanted to destroy me too, rightly so. But, since I rarely interacted with the end user, I only saw what I wanted to see, and ignored the rest."

Being a Husband

"Sabrina brought peace and joy into my life."

The streets of St. Louis were my territory but there was a short period of time, right after graduating high school, that I attended Weber State University in Ogden, UT. It was a culture shock in a good way. Unlike life in St. Louis, I was surrounded by diverse nationalities of people and I enjoyed that. I also started new enterprises while enrolled in school including selling bottles of alcohol to students on campus. It was profitable because I would buy them at the wholesale case price and sell them at a premium to students who had the money and were willing to pay. I did go to class but studying wasn't my biggest priority. During my sophomore year my mother got sick. I was homesick anyway so I was happy to go see about her and be back in St. Louis. Naturally, I picked up my enterprise, and didn't miss a beat. Other than that college experience, I hadn't traveled outside of St. Louis until I met and married my wife, Sabrina.

In the Shoe Store

When I met Sabrina, my brother, Michael, had just died. I was working at Raw Fashion in Northwest Plaza as the manager. Her good friend, Alicia, came in and was looking at a shoe. She was different than most of the other women who came into the store. I could tell by her mannerisms, the way she carried herself and the way she was dressed. Everyone else went to the hoochie momma shoes. She did not. It was a high end Mezlan that caught her eye, made of fine leather with a conservative heel and look. Just by talking to her I could tell that she was a woman of God. Her spirit spoke to me and I just knew it. I told her I would let her buy the shoes on my discount.

She got the pair, and before she walked out, her good friend Sabrina called her. After they talked, Sabrina came up to Northwest Plaza not knowing she was going to be my wife. They went around the corner somewhere and bought me a beginner's Bible and invited me to her church. There were no numbers exchanged but I did go to church that Sunday. Sabrina and her mom were there so I sat with them and enjoyed service. Together we watched Alicia be ordained. It was a touching ceremony and it was good being back in church, especially with Sabrina and her mom next me. We exchanged numbers after service. Sabrina's, conversation was mesmerizing, she was different than others I had dated. She was reserved. She knew things, introduced me to things I never knew. I waited to call her because I didn't want to appear anxious. I wanted to play it right. She called me first.

Later, Sabrina revealed to me a conversation she and Alicia had after meeting me at the shoe store. Alicia told her that if I showed up at church, that we were going to be married.

We dated for a couple of years and married. We got married by her Pastor in her grandmother's huge backyard – about 200 people were there. They talk about that wedding to this day.

My Wife

Sabrina was more educated, more mature and had broader experiences than previous women in my life. It was a refreshing change and I enjoyed the variety of food, activities and travel we experienced as a couple. We had our daughter, Jewel, about a year after we got married and we both settled in to a comfortable life of family, of peace and joy. We did fun things like dancing together. We were great dance partners, as she was the only woman who knew every step I would make and also which way I was going to dip her during our moves. In the summers we enjoyed swimming, outdoor gatherings and wineries. As our baby grew, we enjoyed going on school field trips and watching

Jewel participate in sports. She excelled in rugby, cheerleading and dance classes, not to mention, she was smart and had good grades. We did all we could to give her a safe and loving family environment.

> *"Family life meant the world to me. The closeness and the bond we shared was what I always wanted."*

Big A and Lil' A

*"I knew it was my father as soon as
I saw his face."*

In 2002, when I was 32, my wife and I were together when we ran into my dad at Marshall's on Page Boulevard. I pulled onto the lot and parked in front of a white pearl Cadillac. Impressed with the vehicle, we agreed it was a beautiful car and that the older lady inside seemed to be pretty classy. As we were walking in the door and I looked to my left, I saw a man standing there. I said to Sabrina, "He looks like my dad."

She said, "Yeah, right. Let's get into the store."

I slowed down and said, "No, I'm serious, that's my dad."

She ignored me and I approached him asking, "Is your name Aaron?"

He said, "Yes."

I said, "I'm your son. I'm Lil' Aaron."

My dad looked at me and I looked at him and we both got emotional, a little teary eyed and hugged each other. It felt good to hug my dad. I then introduced him to my wife, who was shocked. It was a beautiful experience.

"How did you know it was him?" she asked. I told her I always had a vision of him in my head. I had seen old pictures of him at my grandmother and aunt's houses all my life, from when we were little kids and my parents were still together. When I saw him, he looked a lot like me, and I just knew it was him, I felt it. Even other customers in the store saw us and were touched by the experience.

Still in disbelief, he told us to follow him outside to meet my stepmom, his wife. When we approached the vehicle, coincidently, it was the pearl Cadillac.

He said, "Carol, this is my son, this is Aaron."

She looked shocked as well, as if to say *I didn't know you had another son.* We all talked on the lot and she hugged me, saying, "It's funny. When you got out of the car earlier, I noticed you and thought you were an attractive young man, now I see where you got your looks from."

We all laughed at that. I looked a lot like my dad, only he was grey. I guess she knew what she liked! We talked for a while longer then exchanged numbers and went inside to finish our shopping.

Bonding with Big Aaron

I remember feeling happy to see my dad, something I had always prayed for. I had asked God many times to see my father before either one of us passed. I knew it was God who had answered my prayers that night. He called me the next day. He said, "Hey fella."

I said, "Hey, how ya doing?"

He invited me over to their house in Hazelwood, about 12 minutes from my house in Florissant, later that day. Of course, I went.

It was a good time because in addition to my dad and his wife, I met several of my siblings and a few nieces and nephews. It was a great visit. Everyone was happy to meet me, and of course, I was happy to meet them. It was also shocking that we both lived in St. Louis County so close to one another yet not aware.

When I told my mother about meeting my dad, she thought it was good and she was happy for us. I had never questioned my mom about my dad and I didn't question him when I met him. To this day I don't know what happened between my parents or why they broke up but I didn't carry bitterness, hostility or any negative feelings toward either of them. I was just joyful to have them and joyful that they were both alive. Two weeks later I picked up my two younger brothers and we met my dad, Carol and the rest of our six siblings they had together at a steak house on Lindbergh Boulevard close to where we lived.

Although we didn't "know our dad," we were joyful to be reconnected with him and to meet his children, our brothers and sisters. It was like a piece of our identities had been given back to us. As the days and months passed, my brothers and I were getting some closure, meeting family members from his side of the family. It was a welcome sense of belonging, especially since we didn't really remember him as little boys. I learned that my dad had worked at the GM Plant on Union in St. Louis City, and then at the plant in Wentzville, for over 30 years, until he retired. He liked playing the lottery and betting on horse races. I would pick him up and we would travel about 35 minutes to Illinois, just crossing the Mississippi River, to hang out together and do what he enjoyed. He liked the Illinois Lottery more than the Missouri Lottery because he won more frequently. We hung out at least three days a week. We had birthday parties together too. My birthday is Nov 18th, his was Nov 19th and Carol's was Nov 20th. It was crazy to me. We all got excited and Carol made sure we had a ball. This went on for years.

Cherishing My Family

Around 2004 or 2005 his brother, my uncle, Walter passed so I road down to South Memphis with my dad, Carol and two of my siblings. Though it was a sad occasion, I got to meet my cousins, Walter's children, and several other relatives. At first it was a bit weird because they didn't know who I was. Then my dad introduced me to the family and that helped a bit. Yet it was strange to meet all of those close relatives who had no clue that me or my brothers existed. After the funeral, we drove back to St. Louis and I continued spending quality time with my dad before he got sick.

Late in 2007, he was admitted to Mercy Hospital in Creve Coeur and diagnosed with stomach cancer. They gave him a colostomy bag and he continued being his laid-back self, assuring me and the rest of us that he was okay. I'm pretty sure he knew that he would leave us soon but he remained calm and helped us feel better about his health.

One day after he got out of the hospital, he took me to meet his older cousin, Rose Jackson, who immediately embraced me. She knew exactly who I was, though I didn't know her. That's when I started meeting her children. It was a huge, loving, warm family of people, my people. Heck, I kind of felt like Antoine Fisher, getting to know my distant relatives. Cousin Rose confirmed what my dad had been telling me – he and I had a lot in common – sharp dressing, good dancers, similar mannerisms, calm demeanor and I really favored him.

In May of 2008, about six months after being diagnosed, my dad started getting sicker. They admitted him to the hospital and then released him shortly after, because there wasn't much more they could do for him. Carol called and said he passed away in their bed about a week later, at the age of 69 years old.

I was hurt because for those years we had built that bond of closeness and then he was gone. I was grateful for those six years we spent, but I wasn't ready for him to go. I was heartbroken.

For so long I had felt a void since my dad hadn't been in my life. Building our relationship meant the world to me. Yet, thankfully with his death, I gained more life, more family. I met his sister, my Aunt Rebecca, who stayed in Chicago, during his funeral proceedings. She was the only one of his siblings still alive. She knew my mother as well. She and her kids showed me and my brothers all love. They knew who we were and hadn't known how to find us. Though I lost my dad, I gained more family and it felt really good to have them because for so long I wanted to know my dad's side of the family. I met so many of my cousins at his funeral, cousins all over the country who I have a bond with today. It felt good to be connected.

At the funeral I also met four more of my siblings – they were older than me and my brothers. They all had the same mother and lived Buffalo, NY and Jacksonville, FL, respectively. It was shocking because they didn't know about me and my younger brothers and we didn't know about them. Once we found out, it was all love. I kind of smile at my dad when I think of that – he had three full families in his lifetime and a legacy of 13 kids. Now, I never run out of relatives to visit.

When people would tell me how much alike we were and I would say, "How could I be like and dress like someone I never knew?" I can admit now, especially as I've matured, that we did have some things in common. My dad, Big Aaron, gave me a lot of love during our short time together and though it felt good, it was too short. I sometimes think of how life might have turned out for me and my siblings if he had stayed with our family, to raise us. That's one of the biggest differences between Big A and Lil' A, I had to be father to my daughters and stay connected to their lives. Knowing the pain of not having a father present made me be 100% committed to being the best father I could, even as I was struggling to be a better man. Through getting to know my dad, I also learned to be a better father.

> *"I believe my Heavenly Father answered my prayers, bringing my earthly father back into my life. I am grateful."*

Hardworking Momma

"Momma used to say, 'I just pray that you get out of that life.' We were close and I'd like to think her prayers helped me change my life."

My mother was a loving, caring woman. When she gave, she gave from her heart. She opened her home to friends and strangers, she cooked if you were hungry, let you bathe if you needed a warm bath and would give a listening ear if you needed to bare your soul. She was kind but direct and she would say what she meant and meant what she said. She didn't hold anything back.

Raising Kids Wasn't Easy

When I was young, my mom knew but she didn't want to know about my activities. She wasn't pleased. She kind of accepted the fact that I was a street hustler, but she also prayed that no harm would come to me. Though I never had a conversation with my mother about my enterprise, I believe she didn't bring it up to me because she probably didn't want to have a confrontation with me about it. I was stubborn and even if she had brought it up, I would not have stopped. When I started giving her expensive things and money when she needed something paid, no questions asked, I think that's when she really knew.

She would always say that she didn't want any harm to come to her kids and that she would rather for us to bury her rather than for her to ever have to bury one of her children. When my brother Michael passed the pain I saw on my mother's face was heartbreaking. To bury her oldest son took so much out of her.

Retirement

After retiring from the Bellefontaine rehabilitation center, I was glad to see my mother enjoy life and have time do to things she loved, like playing Bingo. She also collected elephants, saying they brought her joy and luck. She loved going back home to Mississippi to visit loved ones and friends, especially when she travelled with her mother and her sisters. Throughout the years as she was getting older, her health started declining. She started going in and out of the hospital and taking a lot of medication. She had diabetes, heart and kidney problems, as well as asthma.

Losing Momma

A week before my mother passed, I'll never forget walking into her house and seeing her at the kitchen sink. She had a glow, an indescribable glow. It was almost like God had claimed her already and that angels were surrounding her, waiting to escort her to heaven. My mother called me at 3 o'clock in the morning telling me she was thirsty. She said she wanted a 7UP. I went to the Quick Trip and got her a Sierra Mist because that's all they had. When I walked into the room she was in her bed, happy to see me and to get that soda. Next to her, splayed out on the bed in a heart shape were obituaries of family members. My brother, her brothers, her father and other loved ones, along with her Bible beside her. It was as if she knew her time was about to expire. Seeing her laid out, that woman who carried me for nine months and who did everything for her children. It was so painful. I stayed for a little while and asked if she was alright. She told me that she was, and to go ahead and go to work. I didn't want to leave her but she said, "Boo, go on to work, I'm fine."

When I got to work, something wasn't sitting right with me so I called her house phone, no answer. I called her cell phone, no answer. I repeated, both. No answer. I called my sister to check on momma. When she and my brother got there, she wasn't doing well. They tried to get her out of bed and dressed, but she collapsed in my brother's arms. My niece called me from the hospital and told me to get there right away. When I walked into the room I looked like I was my normal self but I wasn't. Seeing her in that hospital bed. She looked at me and said, "I'm not going to die am I?"

I said, "No Momma, you're going to be alright."

She said, "Baby I'm cold."

A tear ran down her face. She took her last breath and she was gone. I lost it after that. That soda was the last thing my momma ever drank.

Strong and Determined

It wasn't until my grandmother told me many years later that momma had been born with kidney problems and had suffered her whole life with health issues. To see her work and take care of us for all of those years without complaint showed how strong and determined she really was. Thinking of her strength encourages me to keep pushing on, no matter how life twists and turns.

Momma's favorite quote was: *"Love thyself, love thy neighbor, always be a blessing to others and always show respect to the unfortunate."* ~ Odessa Welch

It's been a little over seven years since she passed yet it's hard. I miss her so much. I dread the holidays, as I've lost so much. She was born October 17th, our last meal together was on Thanksgiving and she passed two weeks before Christmas in 2010. I wish I could say it's gotten easier to deal with her loss but that would be a lie. When I lost my mother, I was heartbroken, sad, empty and lonely. She was my comfort zone, the one who put the puzzle together. She always knew when something was wrong with her kids and she would use food to get to the truth (peach cobbler). Part of me died when she died.

> *"If you still have your parents, even if they get on your nerves, go see them, talk to them and spend time with them."*

Love and Loss

"When I changed my life, my heart started to beat again. Though losing loved ones is difficult, it's better than being lost without a beating heart."

Being a husband, I learned to sacrifice, to be responsible and some of the things about manhood I had missed along the way. I was loyal to Sabrina and felt safe with her. I learned to be a responsible man and I straightened up my act. I did not have any extramarital affairs because I was married. I loved and respected her that much not to cheat. I had made a vow to God and I was determined to keep that promise. Though I provided financially for my children, I do regret not having a stable two-parent home for each of them like Jewel experienced as a result of the marriage. I felt blessed that Sabrina welcomed each of my daughters in our lives. We did what we could to spend time with them and participate in their activities. It's just too bad that I didn't turn the corner sooner. Being Sabrina's husband during the good and the bad times gave me joy. When each of us lost close family members, we were there for each other, us against the pain and the loss. I appreciated that.

Though we enjoyed each other, we began drifting apart. After 16 years, our marriage came to an abrupt end. She told me she wanted a divorce. I wasn't prepared for it because we had built what I thought was a comfortable life. When I look back, I think we both started falling out of love but since we had a bond, being together was stable and comfortable. I wasn't going anywhere. At some point, I guess that wasn't enough for her.

The divorce was difficult for me. I didn't want to sign the papers, I didn't want it to end and

I always wished that it was a bad dream from which I would soon awake. It wasn't.

Being Single

Being single was difficult for me, moving into my own one-bedroom apartment after leaving a nice home made me sad and lonesome. I had to rebuild and start over, new life, new experience and new furniture. It was hurtful waking up without her by my side, not seeing her and not tasting her good food – she was an excellent cook. I was lost. I was confused. I was hurting day by day. It was like a pain shooting through my chest that felt as if it would take me out at times. It was just painful. To try and get over the hurt I stayed around people. I kept my two jobs and worked as much as I could to take my mind off of the void of losing my wife and our family. As much as I loved to dance, I avoided it, knowing I didn't have my dance partner in my life anymore. I did my best to get through the months and years, still wanting to wake up from that dream that wasn't a dream.

"My dreams were shattered and my heart was broken, but I was still alive."

Becoming Homeless

"My pride made me homeless."

I was married for so long that when I started dating, it was hard to go back to acting like I was single. I would do things for the women I dated that were reserved for a marriage. I met a woman named Angel who filled a portion of the void my divorce had left. I was at Deja Vu, a local club in St. Louis County, for my brother's birthday get together. When she approached me she said I looked different from the others in the club and that I had a unique style. When she said that I remember being hesitant about getting involved because during that time I was still in love with my ex-wife after being with her for so long. The thought of starting something new was tough and at the same time, a welcome change.

I had really spent too much time hoping and praying we would get back together again for my family's sake. Yet it hadn't happened and after all, it had been six years since we split up.

Then a slow jam came on and Angel and I danced. Afterward, we exchanged numbers. I called a couple days later. We talked on the phone and then the following weekend we met back at the same club to have drinks, though I don't really drink alcohol. We had a good time and continued to see each other regularly.

Things were going pretty good for us. At the time I was living in North County and she lived in an apartment complex about 10 minutes from me with her college-aged daughter. A couple of months after we met she moved into a house in University City, about 30 minutes away. As things progressed, I started spending quality time at her house, keeping my apartment but not being there very often. During the eight months we were dating I purchased a living room, dining room and bedroom set for her. I did this because I was used to being a provider, and I didn't want to sleep in a bed she had been sleeping on with another man. Though her furniture was fine, replacing it made me feel more comfortable being there, she liked the new things, and I felt it was what I was supposed to do as a man since I was over at her place so often.

Being with Angel made me feel good. She had a pretty smile and wore her hair in the traditional Halle Berry style. It was really nice to do activities with her and her daughter, things I had missed doing with my ex-wife and baby girl. What I noticed and didn't like was that she liked to go out and club a lot. We were in our mid 40s and I didn't like doing that, but it was her thing and not mine. Occasionally I went with her but most of the time she would meet her friends and hang out. Though I hadn't yet fallen in love with her, I thought we might have potential for a future.

My Car Was Stolen

On Valentine's morning in 2015, when I woke up and looked outside my window (it was a rare occasion that I had been at my own apartment) my car was gone, with broken glass in its place. I had a red 2007 Chevy Impala LTZ with customized paint, nice rims and upgraded features. I felt heartbroken. After calling the police and making a report, I called and told her my car was stolen. She offered to come and get me. We finished the weekend at her house and then she took me to work on Monday. It took about a week for the police to find the car, across the water, in Cahokia, IL, about 45 minutes from my place. It was completely stripped and the insurance company wrote it off. In the two weeks or so that we were getting through the process and determining which car I would get to replace it, Angel noticeably started getting frustrated with driving me around. I even took cabs a few times just to make it easier on her. One of the last times I was at her house, she had medicine out on the counter, several prescription bottles which, based on their contents, seemed to indicate she may have bipolar personality disorder. It was a little strange because I had never seen these bottles and had never experienced her being extra or short-tempered.

Then, I called and asked if she would take me to work (I was at my apartment that morning) and she said, "Call a cab." I did just that.

I thought that since we were in a relationship that she would be there for me but she wasn't. Things took a turn for the worse when she started back seeing her ex-guy. Once I got my new car, and was leaving her house one morning, there was a note on my car from her ex. It read, "She's playing you to get to spend your money. She's still in love with me. Give me a call." He included his phone number. But when she saw me reading it, she snatched it out of my hands and tore it up right away. I was shocked to see a note on my car. I saw his name before she took it and she denied knowing him. I was suspicious and did some investigating. A couple of times within that week during work hours, I got a company car and drove by her place. Each time I saw a grey SUV parked in her driveway. I knew whose it was because she had pointed it out to me during a conversation when we saw it in the neighborhood. I confronted her and she lied about it. It was over.

I was ready to be done with her but I had some belongings in her house that I couldn't just leave there, especially some personal effects from my mom. Letting go of the relationship wasn't that hard once I saw the truth. From the time of the car being stolen to the time of the insurance company issuing the check and my purchasing the new car was about four weeks. I guess she spent those last two weeks courting him again. It was easy since we didn't see each other much during that time. It was bad enough that she started cheating that quickly, yet that wasn't the worst part of it. It was a letdown to me to have her lie, especially after I did so much for her.

All along the way I was helping her pay bills, again, acting like I was married to her and was responsible for that household. After I had spent the money getting around while I was car-less, paying the down payment for my car, and reviewing all the money I had spent on her, I didn't have enough for me. I had neglected several of my utilities bills, I was behind on my rent and my lease was getting ready to expire. I felt betrayed, hurt and, honestly, I felt afraid that I would be alone again. I didn't get depressed but I shut myself away from a lot of other people because I was hurt and had been scorned, again.

Realizing where I was, and that it was too late to keep my place, I had a couple of options. I could have called a family member or friend to stay with them, there are a couple who would have said yes in a heartbeat; or keep my pride and not call anybody. I was embarrassed about letting myself get in that situation. I chose pride. I cleared out my apartment and put everything I owned in storage and started sleeping in my car. I would park it in front of my sister's house or in front of my job and sleep, getting up extra early to go to 24 Hour Fitness and shower, before going to work. I did this for nearly four months, from March to the beginning of July. Nobody knew.

The first night I slept in my car I couldn't believe I was homeless. It did something to me. It made me think of all I had accomplished and then to have nothing, really messed with my emotions. I worked fulltime during the day so I would wake up at 5:30 a.m., go to the gym to shower to be at work by 7 a.m. After work I would go to random restaurants and eat by myself as if it was nothing. After eating I would drive down by the riverfront, and sightsee but really trying to clear my mind until I started getting sleepy. I would park between 10 p.m. and 1 a.m., depending on how I felt. I would get my pillow and blanket from the trunk and sleep in the backseat when I didn't recline the front sea. It was uncomfortable but I had to sleep in order to work, so I made it work. On paydays I would get a room for three days or so, then back to my car.

I kept my appearance up and I always kept

a smile on my face but nobody ever knew the pain. The pain of losing everything. After having lost my mom, my marriage and having another failed relationship, it took a toll on me. Even to this day it's hard to explain the pain, but by the grace of God I'm getting through it. There were days when I cried. *How could I get myself in this predicament?* During that time, my sister noticed my vehicle in front of her house. She asked me why I was out there and I finally admitted that I was homeless. She couldn't believe it. She immediately invited me into her home and she also said that had she known, I would not have been homeless.

It was my pride that kept me from doing the things that I liked to do. Even though I would get up, shower, go to work, but at the end of the day, I was still alone. I was glad that my sister and her husband let me stay. Being around family felt good but it still made me realize how I was missing my own family. I am so blessed to have a loving family who was willing to overlook how far I had fallen. I was grateful that they would accept me no matter what situation I was in. As I'm writing I'm thinking about how angry my Ace was, when he found out that I had been homeless, telling me I could have come to his house no matter what.

Going through that made me stand strong and made me believe that God was good. I could have gotten frost bite, someone could have run into the car while I was sleeping, on rainy nights, tree branches could have fallen on the car, I could have been robbed, my car could have gotten stolen again, and I could have been living in the car more than those four months. My sister noticing and offering me a place to live was the only thing that got me out of my car because even though I was down, I would never have asked for help or revealed what was really happening. I guess part of it is that all of these years I had been a private person, especially because of my early enterprises, and also because I prided myself on being a provider, always there for everyone else.

I feel like God has a call on me because He brought me through so much and made me a whole new person and that He's not done with me. There is more for me to do. Living in St. Louis is home, it will always be home. But, when I've gone to other places like Dallas and Denver, I've been embraced by extended family and it feels so good – the people, the diversity, the way they treat me. I feel like my journey, or at least the next part of my journey is somewhere else. I have to get out and venture, to see where God is leading me, to my destiny.

> *"I'm a family guy. I miss the family life. I need the warmth of children, I enjoy being in the father role. I don't have all of the answers, but I know there are better days ahead for me."*

Epilogue

Though it may be hard to believe me if you don't know me, I have a heart for others. I want people to know that everything you think you want is not all it's cracked up to be – especially the material things. They don't last. I had put those things before God. He took them away. Today, I feel good about the changes in my life.

Writing this book was important because I wanted to tell my story, something I had been holding onto for so long. Everything on the outside looked good, but the inside was torn apart. I want people to know that if I could make a change from the lifestyle, others can make a change as well.

Right before I started writing this book I found out from my cousin that my grandmother used to pray for me to get out of the life. She prayed that something would happen to me – enough to stop – but not enough to take me out. She and my mother had many sleepless nights worrying about me. At the time, I didn't understand the bigger picture of my actions. I felt that having money to take care of things was most important and I wasn't trying to hear or see differently. My grandmother knew I was stubborn, prideful and a hard worker. She also knew I had a heart beneath all of my toughness. I'm so grateful for my praying grandmother. When I heard about what she did and said, it made me feel good, loved and joyful that she got on her knees and thanked God that nothing happened to me. The thought of that overwhelmed me and confirmed that I was loved. My grandmother just turned 94 years old. Especially since my parents have gone on, having her alive and kicking is priceless.

In my early life I did things to survive and because I wanted the material things that money could buy. I was enticed by money, jewelry, women and power. I changed my life because I started seeing things differently. The wrong priorities had consumed me. With experience and maturity I realized I had to get out of survival mode if I was going to live. And having material possessions wasn't as important as they once were. It took death, darkness and danger for me to decide peace of mind was more important. If you're struggling with something in your life, it's never too late to stop or to make a change. Please remember that, and don't let your pride or fear stop you from being a better you.

There is no price tag you can put on peace of mind, a healthy, beating heart or on the love of family and friends. Not looking over my shoulder, going to my tax payer job and feeling good about encouraging others makes me feel good and I'm grateful for the change.

What I most want today, at almost 50, is to be married again, have a family, travel and go places with my spouse, enjoying the moments. I'm looking forward to the joy and love we will share.

I've been thinking about where I want to go next. My daughters are grown and it seems like the West is calling me. We'll see where I land but right now, I still call St. Louis my home. Thanks for reading *Street Glory, The Untold Story.*

God bless you all.

Discussion

There are many conversations to be had about Fatherhood, Marriage and God.

Maybe would could talk about them in person one day?

Until then, here are some of my thoughts for your consideration because we have to take responsibility for our actions, and the way we affect others, especially our family members, so that they get there is something to follow...

Fatherhood

"Missing my father and becoming a father shaped my life and choices."

Not Having My Father Affected Me More than I Knew

1. Seeing other kids' dads around/activities was difficult and made me sad, wondering where he was, who he was and what life would be like if he was around.

2. Not having his presence nor a relationship in the same home definitely impacted our home-life. Since our mother was working so much to support us, we got into things that kids do when a father-figure is absent.

3. Missing male role models – My older brother, Michael, did his best to help us, his three younger brothers become men. But when he left, I was young and headed in another direction. We as men/young men are always role models – however, the direction we head in may not always be a good one. With that being said, it's important for boys and girls to have a strong, positive male influence to teach them, lead them and to protect them.

Because I didn't have a father figure in my life as a young man, I knew the importance of being present for my own children. Long before I chose to settle down and be married, I created daughters who needed me. I wanted them to understand that I would be there for them – through the thick and thin, and that no matter what, I was going to make sure they were well-taken care of.

If you have children, be a stand-up dad and be present with your children during their activities, be reliable, get in the habit of helping them set goals while they are young, make sure you give them love and attention. Our youth today really need more guidance.

Being Married

"I did not have any extramarital affairs because I loved her that much not to cheat on her. I made that vow to her, under God and I meant it."

Cheating Is Easy

Now that you've read my book, you know I was a ladies man in my younger years. It was easy and I enjoyed the thrill of having multiple women. As I matured, I slowed down, but I didn't stop until I got married. There are a lot of people who cheat while married. Most people cheat because they aren't getting attention at home.

A lot of men will go outside of marriage for sexual pleasure and for freakier things, even if they have a loving wife at home, feeling like she's not doing the things the outside chick is doing. Many women go outside of the home because they don't feel appreciated, loved or supported by their spouse. You've got to have loyalty, trust, and a solid foundation. A woman wants stability. She has to know she's in her comfort zone with her husband – that she is his everything.

Build and maintain a covenant of love, embracing each other, stay aware of each other's needs, as they change over time, and never let the torch, flame burn out – catch it and keep it going when it starts to flicker.

God's Grace

"Though I'm not a 'Holy Roller' I am a believer in God and I give all credit and praise to Him."

Even when I was hustling, I believed in God. The issue was that I made material things more important than His presence. However, I know without Him I would not be alive today. As I am looking over my life, I have peace of mind, I feel blessed to be alive and I am enthusiastic to be able to share things from my heart and life to encourage others. I credit God for saving me when I could have easily been consumed by the lifestyle I was leading and I thank Him for giving the chance the change.

1. **There is always hope.** There is always a better day and a better tomorrow if you trust and believe in His will.

2. **You can always change.** I am truly blessed to have experienced the things I have in life that made me into a wiser, better person. Since I could change, I know anyone can change, if they desire to do so.

3. **Your lifestyle is your choice and comes with certain risks and benefits.** I feel at ease and at peace that I don't have to worry about looking over my shoulders anymore; or that someone is trying to hurt me or to take away things I have worked for.

4. **Family is everything, don't take them for granted.** Being embraced by family makes me humble and I do my best to be there for everyone.

5. **Your legacy matters.** I am far richer today, wealthy in the things that matter,

than I was when I had pockets full of money, living a dangerous lifestyle. It feels good to contribute to people rather than to take away or hurt them through my endeavors. I'm grateful.

6. **Expanding your horizons means growth and new opportunities. Through the ups and downs, Our Savior will turn it all around.** God is directing me on another path to see things, allowing me to travel, and experience things I've never seen and to go places I've never been. It's not too late. It's exciting. You can do it too.

"But rise and stand upon your feet,
for I have appeared to you for this purpose,
to appoint you as a servant
and witness to the things in which you
have seen me and to those in which I will appear to you, delivering you from your people and
from the Gentiles—to whom I am sending you
to open their eyes, so that they may turn from darkness to light and from
the power of Satan to God,
that they may receive
forgiveness of sins and
a place among those who are sanctified
by faith in me."

Acts 26:16-18

About the Author

Aaron Welch grew up in St. Louis, Missouri, the fifth of seven kids by his mother. When his parents split up, his mom, who was in the nursing profession, began working two jobs to support the family because of her commitment to providing. Each sibling "lead the younger ones" until they left the home. When it was his turn, Aaron had already been captivated by movies like *Scarface*, *Superfly* and *The Mack*, as well as TV shows like *Miami Vice*, each glorifying street life. He tried it, he liked it and he was hooked on being a player in the game. He began to hustle as a young, quiet teenager, building a successful empire within the confines of his territory in 'the City.' One fight in 9th grade changed the course of his life as he was "sent" to 'the County' to stay out of trouble. That move didn't work, it simply increased his opportunity and built new relationships. With the changing times and increased danger, along with the effects of his choices coming to light, he stopped.

Author **Aaron Welch** is the proud father of five daughters. Adjusting to life in a lower tax bracket, he decided his family, safety, peace of mind and heart were more important than the temporary satisfaction found in money, women, cars and **Street Glory.**

www.ingramcontent.com/pod-product-compliance
Lightning Source LLC
Chambersburg PA
CBHW071113030426
42336CB00013BA/2070